THE PENTATHLON

OF FIVE DIFFERENT ARTICLES

DR GNANASEKARAN

ISBN 979-888503009-0

to my brother

Contents

CHAPTER ONE

PRACTICING ENGLISH LANGUAGE: SIGNIFICANCES AND SERIOUSNESSES

English is the most popular language in the world. If we practice it, we can get in touch with anyone in any country. This is possible because English is international and spoken in more than 106 countries. So, where do we start practicing English on our own? Of course, practising the English language as a second language is a complex and structured process. It is difficult to master science subjects independently, but if we know how to start practising English on our own, we can cope with the task. In the modern world, the importance of English knowledge is undeniable, so more and more people are trying to master this language. However, many beginners who have not studied English before are lost by a variety of methods and textbooks. Practicing English anew is not that difficult if we know where to start and how to use it. In this article, we are going to have some important tips for practicing English to the beginners.

What do we need to learn a language?

To learn the basics of English for tourism purposes, a self-study guide and a dictionary with basic words and phrases will suffice. If our goal is universal, we need a quality dictionary, grammar book and various audio and video lessons in English. It is a well-known fact that the best way to become proficient is to communicate with our people. If we have the opportunity to chat with any native English speaker, use should use it. Alternatively, it is apposite to watch English films without dubbing (subtitles are acceptable) or to read English fiction in English. Make sure we have a new note book in which we can write new words and practice them all in our daily situations.

Setting a goal:

Once we have determined what level of English we need and how much we need to learn new words and rules at the right time, we are ready to set goals. Reaching each new small goal, we gradually cross the path of practicing new English. Each new step gives us a new level. If we set an approximate time scale, it will apply:

- Learn the whole alphabets in 2 weeks.
- Learn the acceptable pronunciation in 3 weeks.
- Learn the basics (present, past and future) in 1 month.
- Minimum vocabulary in 50 days - 300 words or more.

Surround ourselves with English:

We need to fill the space around us with an English speaking ambience. For example, hanging leaflets in the apartment with new words and can listen to the news in BBC English. We can also find a foreign friend who can chat with us on Facebook every day. Oral and written training in English can be made possible through various websites. If we have an opportunity to go abroad, it will be our most informative and interesting trip because we will have the opportunity to immerse ourselves in the English atmosphere without artificially creating it.

Maintaining motivation:

Mastering the English as a second language is not an easy task. After one or two classes, we may feel that these terms and exceptions are never subject to us. Now we have to think of those who started and advanced as we did. We can also do it too, yes we should trust ourselves. Curiosity about the subject is the key to our success. One needs English for work, another for travel, and one-third for self-improvement. Each has its offers, but it is the best if there are several.

Starting English Practicing:

If we decide to practice English anew, we need to go from simple to complex sentences and from very essential to the hard. First, we should try to lay the foundation for future knowledge and skills and practice the basics of the language. The most basic rules are as follows:

- Practicing alphabets.
- Reading the rules - can read words aloud.
- Pronunciation - Words can be read aloud so it becomes clear.
- Basic Glossary - This is usually said to be 500 to 3000 common words.
- Minimal grammar - without it we cannot add words to sentences.

Reading:

Undoubtedly first, we will have to familiarize ourselves with the rules, examples and simple texts. Reading grammatically correct sentences will give us a better result – in fact there is a skill of memorizing vocabulary and grammatical constructions through reading. Visual activity is the main source for attaining new information, and it is essential to read English texts regularly at any stage of language practicing.

Listening:

When practicing the English language anew, it may seem impossible to understand the text by listening alone. This can be a great support to read. A pronunciation application can help us imitate how to pronounce a particular sound or word. If we read the text with our eyes and listen to it at the same time, we can have two mangoes with one stone. It gradually expands the boundaries of our knowledge, and makes us listening to the text again. At first, we will only understand a few words, then sentences. This is the only way to learn listening, which still plays a significant role in practicing English language. Listening to English language songs and watching movies, including subtitles, supports the beginners and enhances motivation by immersing them in real life situations without any interruption. It will be very useful to watch our favourite movies in English language, which we are familiar with in our mother tongue. Thus, these familiar storytelling activities will make us comprehend the characters in English more vividly.

Writing:

Any new thoughts and feelings must be created in writing. The system of writing in a regular notebook can be very effective in practicing the language and the effectiveness of the written exercises allows us to develop our knowledge and bring it to an automated level. First, we will learn how to express our thoughts correctly on paper so that we can confidently use them all in our daily speech.

Speaking:

Spoken training is an integral part of practicing a language. Reading and translating a language do not mean that we can speak English fluently. Fluency is the dream of any beginner, but to fulfill it, we need to engage upon it constantly. If we do not have a trainer, better we can train ourselves. For example, we can speak in front of a mirror on how our day has gone. We can also go through a new topic, find a new name, even we can create a fictional character. These best practices that are made into reality after speaking will give us a diverse knowledge on oral topics. We can achieve even greater success by connecting what we read or what we listen. After we read the text or listen to the audio recording, we can imitate the content aloud. A representation like this can help training memory and thinking and teach us to reconsider in our own words and, therefore, we can speak English fluently.

Dictionary:

The study of vocabulary in a foreign language begins with simple and frequently used terms:

- Nouns (e.g. a house, a man, an apple)
- Adjectives (e.g. big, good, beautiful)
- Verbs (e.g. run, go, sleep)
- Pronouns (e.g. I, he, she)
- Numbers (e.g. one, ten, fifth)

For those who want to practice English, thoughtless blockage is not suitable. Undoubtedly, international words are remembered very quickly, and the rest are better combined with the already familiar lexical units. Continuous expressions produced in English language are neatly remembered for example, "A big dog" and "An interesting movie". When memorizing these lexical units, special attention should be paid not only to their meaning but also to their pronunciation. That is why it is important to learn exactly how to interpret a word transcript accurately at an early stage of practicing English and to learn the pronunciation rules of certain letter combinations, for example, "th" and "ng".

Grammar:

The time for grammar comes when we read English language and write their basic vocabulary. But we should not immediately drown us in this topic. All we need now is to learn how to make simple sentences correctly. To get started in English language at home, it is enough to master ourselves with the 3 tenses (present simple, past simple, future simple) and having regular practice on the word formation. As we learn the simple past tense, we will find that some verbs make the past different from others. These verbs are called irregular, and every form of them must be memorized. Each of these elements is important, so that we cannot miss anything because these points are all interrelated. We should also not to forget the fact that it is difficult for us to understand the language without proper pronunciation. Even if we learn the whole dictionary, we will not speak, because the sentences are structured according to certain rules, we need at least a basic knowledge of grammar to produce them correct, because speech is not just a bunch of words.

Online Dictionaries and British Council's Exercises:

Online dictionaries are useful for beginners and translators. For each word, dozens of meanings and standard phrases in English are given there. It is one of the great ways to learn English on our own. Through these websites or applications, students regularly practice lessons containing theory, tests, practical exercises, and game assignments. In addition to the standard theoretical rules, we can also practice the British English which is centered upon the British Council's online worksheets and exercises. There are also video materials, podcasts, songs and games in English that can be easily understood in the beginning.

Ways to learn English quickly:

As practice shows, people are stuck in uncomfortable situations due to lack of competence of the English language. We have to practice the language as part of the school curriculum, but the knowledge gained in our schools is not enough for communication and work. Now, many learners are trying to understand this matter seriously. It is easy to practice any foreign language in a country where its speakers speak their mother tongue, for instance England. But not everyone can leave the homeland for such a big purpose.

1. If we can't make a short trip to England or the US, please recreate the English-speaking environment at home.
2. Learn phrases in the language we learn every day. Prefer complex phrases, explaining the proverb or the speech of some great personalities.
3. Write each phrase in a notebook, rewrite it several times, print it on paper and hang it on the refrigerator door or in another prominent place. Speak the learned things aloud through right pronunciation.
4. Surround ourselves with English. It should be with us everywhere. Listening to music or reports in a foreign language may not make any sense to us at first. Then, we

can catch the usages as understandable phrases.

5. Download the original English language series on our computer. Before going to bed, browse the series and discuss it with our family members the next day.

A good start does not always guarantee a good end, so the system of an independent research should be approached responsibly. Remember that this is what we need first, and we will have all the control over the course of the company and its results.

- Practice regularly.
- Set ourselves the required duration of classes, for example, at least 30 minutes a day 3 times a week.
- Choose tasks at our level to avoid disappointing ourselves and our skills. If we already have some knowledge, we can rewrite short texts, translate texts or articles, and find a speechwriter to practice speaking skills.
- All the acquired knowledge should be put into practice immediately, while all vocabulary and grammatical constructions should be used in both oral and written speech.

Now it is easy to decide where to start practicing English on our own. If we know the language, we can communicate with foreign friends and colleagues and draw information from indescribable English language sources.

Tips for Practicing the English Language:

1. Collect all the necessary stationery items.
2. Take notes by hand through simple words and simple sentences.

3. Spell everything we put in the notebooks.
4. Check ourselves daily: Writing from memorized words, rules, sentences and poems.
5. Avoid distractions and breaks in the language practicing classes. It is important to pay full attention.
6. Create a personal syllabus for ourselves. Even if we decide to study independently, we must adhere to the given table so that we can go with the planned syllabus carefully and thoughtfully over a fixed period.
7. Try to practice English slowly. Good academic courses focus not on speed, but on the effectiveness and quality of training because we always forget the things we have learned quickly and we will have to train again in the future.
8. Take rest at least one day a week. However, long breaks should not be done through vacations. Instead, we can take books, posts and CDs with us.
9. Keep in touch with exercises even on weekends.
10. Take some books in English and gradually translate them into our mother tongue.
11. Follow and remember the patterns that make up most phrases through sentences, links between the characters in the stories and the usage of the words and the semantic logic of the stories.
12. Read English Poems and their Translations.
13. Listen to classical music in English and practice to understand foreign speech well. We can also watch English TV channels: When listening to news programs, we will be trained in the ability to differentiate English speech. Thus, we will gradually become accustomed to listening and understanding texts in a foreign language.
14. Develop the ability to write and speak. Spend at least 30 minutes of training each day. Describe objects, events

and happenings in English. Talk about celebrities, movies and books, our friends and relatives in English. Pronounce each word carefully and use vocabulary that we can remember. Gradually, we will test ourselves independently and learn to fill in the gaps in practice.

15. Speak English and record our speech. Compare with models of training campuses. So we can find our flaws, weaknesses and improve pronunciation. Sometimes it is best if we have the opportunity to communicate with a native speaker of a foreign language. He can edit us and give advice.
16. Pay special attention to grammar, vocabulary, and pronunciation. Practice the English words carefully. Build our vocabulary skills regularly and repeat the words of different thematic groups daily.
17. Stop going to Spoken English courses. Instead, we can learn semantics, especially verbs
18. Stop being ashamed of our mistakes since we are all learners till the death.
19. Watch our favourite TV shows and movies in English. Try to understand them all through the subtitles first, then without. Do not try to translate every word instead understand the general meaning.
20. Travel a lot and surround ourselves with interesting people who do not speak our mother tongue (international companies, online communities, for example, online chat with foreigners).

Works Cited:

Bolinger, Dwight. *Aspects of language.* New York: Harcourt, Brace & World Inc. M.N.K. (2007).

Jalaluddin, NorHashimah& et al. "Linguistics and environment in English language learning: Towards the development of quality human capital". European Journal of Social Sciences, 9(4), 27-642, (2009).

James, Cherian. "An analysis of selected problems that confront students and teachers of second language". *Dissertation Abstracts International*, 57(9), 3857- A. (1996).

Nunan, D. The impact of English as a global language on educational policies and practices in the Asia-Pacific region. TESOL Quarterly, 37 (4), 589-613. (2003).

CHAPTER TWO

STORYTELLING FOR KIDS AND THE ROLE OF TEACHERS IN CHILD PROTECTION

Introduction

There are many teaching methods for teaching social sciences to elementary and middle school students. They are game, acting, questioning, environmental context, verbal, textbook, project, detection, group teaching, planning learning, puzzles solving, conversation and storytelling respectively. Among them, the art of storytelling is the taking of events and messages.Storytelling is the process of emotionally expressing the events in a subject according to imagination, creativity, body, age, and liking.In this article,we can see how a story can make a positive difference in a student's mind.

Types of stories

- True stories

- Fiction
- Myths

True stories

True stories tell the true story of birds, animals, plants, vines, the sky, the earth, the planets, natural systems, human food, clothing, relationships, and living conditions. Places where people live, climate, climate, natural systems such as rivers, lakes, lakes, oceans, depths, mountains, valleys, continents, natural changes in them, eruptions, industries, yield crops, how they were used and how they developed in each period. And the living conditions of the people can also be told through true stories. Stories help to stimulate students' imagination, develop cognitive knowledge, and enhance memory.

Telling subjects as stories

Our country's warriors, heroic deeds, legends, kings' ways of ruling, reforms, the benefits and disadvantages of them, how they contribute to the actions of the state in the present and know the consequences, etc., can know the challenges facing the country. It creates a sense of 'we can'. The services rendered by man to the country then and the duties to be performed by every citizen to the country today, birth, death, population, population control, health, cleanliness, civic, cultural, maintenance, safety, scientific and technological development when told through stories take the true position for each student. That being said, story events can help bring about behavioral change among students.Seafaring, new discoveries, space exploration, the exploration of explorers' heroism, self-confidence, and the work they have done for the people of the world and their countrymen (e.g., the discoveries of Magellan, Columbus, Vasco da Gama and Vespucci) can induce the students being more imaginative. Stories about astronaut KalpanaChawla and astronaut SunitaWilliams, will no doubt inspire students' knowledge and curiosity and take them to the next level of achievement. Therefore, it can be said that true stories take the best place in the subject.

Fiction

Fictions are about a person who does not exist, an animal, a forest, a place, a town, a country and it contains unheard of deeds that we do not see. Similarly there are fictions based on a true incident. It contains imagination, metaphor, metaphor, and beautiful poetic style. For example, it is like "The diamond ornaments lying on the ground were smashed by lightning into". Unseen monsters, stories of spells, spells and tricks.

Myths

The myths are set in the most remote places unknown to the student, with religious myths in the background, and the kings of the time explaining the constitution. The stories depict the qualities of human love, affection, devotion, friendship, valour, and compassion, as well as anger, greed, harm to others, and the devastation that results. Students are able to learn through religious stories that the highest purpose of human life is to worship the sheets of God. These help to develop human qualities. We can see the concept behind the myths in today's practice as well. For example in the scene where Rama fights with Ravana in the Ramayana, when Ravana fights, he is broken and he stands unarmed. Then Rama said to Ravana, "Go today and come tomorrow." The show is a perfect example of the character that is displayed to the enemy on the battlefield as well.

Pictures in stories

Collecting materials according to the syllabus set according to the social science curriculum of elementary, middle school, and students.

- Images and Pictures
- Posters
- Series Image Cards
- Paintings
- Booklet

Can be collected and used to make the story more interesting and attractive.

Land maps: Places where historical events are told

- Routes,
- States,
- Seas,
- Islands,
- Forest,
- Mountains,
- Rivers,
- Mountains,
- Historical wars,
- Temples of historical significance,
- Places where important leaders were born and lived,
- Conferences, places of agreement,
- Areas considered miracles.

Photos:

- Parliament,
- Assembly,
- National and local festivals,

- Country Troops,
- Community sculptors,
- National Security,
- Heads of State,
- Natural resources,
- Regional,
- State-wise monuments

Can be collected as photographs and tell stories about the topography of the place, major industries, exports, imports, their background, importance in the form of stories.

Land Maps

In the land map drawn on the banks of the Jhelum, Alexander and the Indian emperor recounted a battle, and King Purusottama jumped on a horse called "Chetak" to save him from the river, and we still see the name "Satak" in two-wheeled vehicles. Can be immersed. Alexander's warlords made false noises as they descended into the Jhelum River and threw fireballs. Believing it to be true, Alexander disbanded Porus‘ elephants as he advanced. Students will enjoy watching the show through their maps.

Method of using images

- Images for teaching social sciences should be used at all stages of the lesson (learning steps)
- Only pictures of a subject should be used for teaching.
- Encourage a sense of truth in history, civics and geography and give explanations to them.
- Why? What? How? Why? How? The pictures should be arranged in such a way as to answer the questions.
- Teachers should prepare students to set appropriate titles, descriptions, chronological order, use of

appropriate colours, and appropriate educational use for use by all students.

The role of the teacher in teaching

- Teachers should follow the oral teaching method to tell stories to primary school students.
- Design stories that fit the subject.
- Legends, true stories, myths, stories from magazines can be told if they are suitable for the subject.
- The teacher should tell the story in simple words packed with meaning that students can understand. Stories should be interesting.
- The lesson is captivating when the author expresses the emotions of the characters through narration, parable, comparison, etc. through the voice, down, laughter, joy, affection, compassion, friendship, valour, determination. Teaching using finger, hand, and body movements with verbal variations when the author is expressing specific opinion, word concept, general rules, and reflecting neural emotions will result in an off experience such as the characters in the story speaking to the listeners. Telling the story of the freedom fighters of the Indian colony in the form of archery, storytelling and song will cultivate patriotism among students.

Elements of the story

- Language
- Gestures
- Music
- Facial expressions

For the author's words and verses, for example VeerapandiyaKattabomban's"to whom you ask Tax" should be said.Ashoka'sKalinga war scene should arouse the interest of the students by uttering phrases such as "People's pleasure, king's pleasure".The teacher's mimicry of Bird, animal, thunder, wind, lightning, rain in many voices, differentiating the raising and lowering the sound helpthe students to imprint in the mind with the same feeling the ideas that were brought. Gestures expressed through bodily movements reveal action, command, and obligation.Facial expressions with many emotions give strength and brilliance to the conversation.

Elementary middle schools teachers can tell stories and take the messages they tell for discussion. E.g. Students can be asked to imagine the first Indian freedom struggle in India, - as if it had been a success. Patriotism, thoughts and peace prevail among the students through the heroic and patriotic expressions of the teacher as he carries out the subject matter in a narrative manner.

The teacher must complyto:

1. Preparation according to age / class
2. Face to face
3. Providing with appropriate changes in feelings / facial / body language
4. Knitting stories to arouse interest

Each individual has an opportunity to find problems and find solutionsif they are taught world culture, society, biology, history, war, environmental pollution, women's advancement, creatures, the challenges faced by the people and the knowledge of family traditions in the form of stories.

How should the stories unfold?

Simple dialogue and limitedcharacterizationwill help developing student competence. The story should be based on human qualities such as love, valor, virtue, justice and self-confidence.

Characteristics of storytelling

1. Emotional
2. Exploring problems
3. Achieving learning objectives
4. Duty in society
5. Eliminate caste, religion and ethnic differences
6. Giving happiness.
7. Giving humour
8. Learning readiness / song / drama skill development
9. Encouraging language development. Storytelling helps to acquire all life skills and values, apart from being cohesive and motivating.
10. Sociology teaching can make the subject more palatable, attractive, and vibrant.
11. Imagination helps students to develop creative activities.
12. Story transforms students into character and personality.
13. Stories related to heritage, mythology, true fiction, foreign affairs, heroism and research that are supposed to entertain the students' minds are the cultural highlights of the country and abroad. They are the priceless high treasures of the people of the country if not superfluous.
14. Students will be motivated to learn more about history, civics, and geography when they are told in a way that explains real events.
15. Therefore, students will seek to compare the life, social, economic, political and religious conditions of the people of ancient, medieval and modern times, to know

their specialties and to see their development in the present. Develop better engagement, courage and vision among students.

The importance of questioning in storytelling

During the storytelling, the teacher asks the students questions in the middle, which stimulates the students' interest in the subject through interpersonal relationships, story performances, and emotional interpretations.Helps students develop their natures. (E.g.) Stories that focus on truth, honesty, heroism, and aesthetics can cause behavioural change among students if they are to illustrate virtues. When Mahatma Gandhi, Nehru and Netaji stories are told with life events, social reforms, local, regional and state historical background, the stories will help them to understand and act on the importance of the problems that have arisen from time to time and to engage themselves in them. But the teacher owes much to bringing about such a change.

Discussions and the questions that arise through them will help to know the true situation and to know the pros and cons of the situation. It is acceptable to arrange the quiz sequence in such a way as to enable each student to focus, speak, and express his or her ideas when the teacher asks questions.

1. Teacher Question: The whole class participates
2. Teacher Questioning: Small group participation in two rows or class
3. Teacher Questioning: A student's participation
4. Student Questioning: Participation of students.

Evaluation in storytelling

Stories help students' talents and personality development to go straight. When we listen to stories we learn about the actions and achievements of those who lived among us, our ancestors, and today's generation. They also seek to compare them to today's situation. Realize how we use them for the betterment of the individual and the nation.The teacher uses simple words, words, phrases, metaphors, or illustrations to suit the character.Narrative films and collections illustrate the political, social and economic developments that took place during the story. It encourages students to produce pictures, drawings and photo galleries in parallel. These will help to develop students' imagination, creativity and individual student skills. The textbooks are converted into stories so that they can be remembered for a long time.

Child Protection

Wherever children are, they suffer from neglect, and abuse. They can also be bullied in some way at school. Homes can be subject to similar atrocities. The child in your class may have been the victim of bullying and exploitation outside of school. You should not ignore it. In other words, you need to help them. Whenever you can do this, you must first identify if the child is suffering from a problem like this. You have to spend the necessary time to understand it. We need to think about the mechanism of what can be done to solve them. Do not think that it is your duty to save the children until they come to school. Your intervention can make a huge difference in the life of a child who cannot afford school life. All you need to do is give them an outlet and the support they need to keep going. You need to learn more about their problem and think about what you can do to solve them. If you decide mentally, you can make the necessary arrangements and means to shore up the problem. Thus, you can achieve things that you never even dreamed you could do.

Are you a teacher who is friendly with children?

If you do the following, you can become such a teacher.

- Understand that children's rights are also human rights. Create such an understanding in the society in which you live.
- Make children realize that being in your classroom can be very rewarding.
- Be open-minded about learning new things
- Be a friend, and mentor to the child.
- Take a tasty lesson. Tell students a lot of useful information
- Create opportunities for children to ask questions and doubts.
- Practice recognizing and realizing many disabilities such as being bullied, neglected, and having difficulty in learning.
- Practice with children so that they can express different feelings such as their opinions, worries, benefits and tragedies. Talk to them about normal things as well.
- Learn to take good care of yourself and discuss with your children the problems they face at school and at home.
- Understand the things that can affect a student's life.
- In such cases, make sure they develop their skills to attend in a way that is beneficial.
- Have students discuss with school management and arrange meetings accordingly.
- Organize discussions at parent-teacher association meetings about existing rights for children.
- Decide not to inflict corporal punishment. In any case, understand the need for children to be restrained by using methods such as speaking and comforting.

- Protest against discrimination. Establish good relationships with children from minority and backward students.
- Stop saying negative things about working children. Likewise, stop citing the negative examples of street children, children who have been sexually abused, abductions, domestic violence, child abuse, and many other children who need protection in the society.
- Stop using child labour in your home and workplace.
- Do not act without structure while acting democratically.
- Take care not to harass children not only in school but also in their communities.
- If such a situation arises, do not hesitate to call the police / take legal action.
- Encourage children to take their ideas to the adults in their respective communities.
- Give children the responsibility of organizing events. Give them responsibilities and guide them to fulfil them.
- Take the children to important places on the side, and to tourist sites.
- Encourage children to participate in discussions, question-and-answer sessions and meaningful entertainment.
- Ensure that girls are educated in new ways, with mindfulness in the classroom.
- Find out thedropped out girls who come under dropouts of school and girls who take frequent breaks from class so that they do not continue to take leave.
- Definitely possible if all teachers work hard to help create a safe environment around children.
- Your attention span is very important. Only by paying close attention can you accurately assess the growth and

progress of the children in your class. If you find that something is wrong, then your next step should be to find out what the cause is.

- Next, ask the question of whether the child in question is being harassed in any way by family, friends, relatives, etc., and seek answers.
- Explain the child's problems in some way. Encourage the child to express his or her problems through writing, colouring, painting, or story writing. Talk to yourself or to a school counsellor, friend or social worker.
- See if sex education can be taught by taking into account the age and maturity of the children.
- Tell children about HIV / AIDS. Tell them about how this disease affects and spreads to an individual. Also tell them what to do to prevent these from happening.
- In the classroom, make sure that those who are infected and those who are suffering from the disease are not branded or isolated in any way.
- Creating and strengthening a safe environment for children is an activity that requires work from many levels. For this, collaboration, coordination, and doing so by sharing what is known to both parties, etc., are essential.
- Traditional methodologies, attitudes, etc. are essential when doing these. Basic needs include providing services, monitoring them, and identifying individuals who are working for their advancement.
- Teachers need to know what the government plans for children and what the benefits are. We need to identify children and families who are in a position to benefit from such schemes of the government. The list of such children and families can be submitted to any of the local, taluk and zonalpanchayat members in your area.

If you want to save children who are affected or vulnerable, it is essential to keep in touch with the following government officials.

- Police
- Your panchayat / municipality, mayor and member.
- Anganwadi staff
- Members of Regional / Taluka / Zonal and District Panchayats.
- Regional Development Officer or Panchayat Officer
- District Judge / Head of District Administration (IAS Officers – Disctrict Collector)
- Office or Officer of the Child Welfare Committee nearest to your area.
- Child helplines in your area.

Ways to identify children who have been sexually abused.

Signs found in children and adolescents who have been sexually abused

Girls of 6-11 years old

- Being sexually explicit in behaviour when interacting with other children
- Describing the sexual abuse she experienced
- Excessive concern about the genitals
- Sexual identification of older persons and reference to the relationship pattern
- Sudden expression of fear or apprehension about women, men or specific places
- Being aware of adult sexual behaviours
- Sleep problems, changes nightmares and panic attacks

Girls of 12-17 years old

- Having sex with children younger than herself, trying to persuade them to comply with her wishes
- Exposing sexuality in behaviour or avoiding things about sexuality altogether
- Problems with food intake
- Attempts to distance oneself from feelings of guilt, shame, and humiliation
- Running away from home

Boys of 6-11 years old

- Being sexually explicit in behaviour when interacting with other children.
- Sudden fear of men, women or certain places
- Sleep problems, nightmares, screaming in sleep
- Suddenly rudely behaving or pretending to be a particular person
- Not liking already favourite things
- Exposure to childish behaviours

Boys of 12-17 years old

- Having sex with children younger than himself, trying to persuade them to comply with his wishes
- Sudden childish behaviour
- Behaving like certain people, deliberately engaging in dangerous things
- Attempts to free himself from feelings of guilt, shame, and shame

Precautions:

The signs or symptoms mentioned above are a sign that a child is in trouble and may be sexually abused. If a child has any of these symptoms, it should not be concluded that the child has been sexually abused. Only if there are many signs and symptoms, should such a conclusion be reached. Evaluate your intuition in this. Children should always listen to adults and walk.They are raised with the instruction to obey. This society suggests that this is how children should behave, even if they do not like the behavior of adults. Children tend to forget to deny it when adults behave in a way that they do not like or accept. In such a situation, children need to be taught to say no.

Ten Commandments on How to Treat Children with Disabilities

I. Children with physical disabilities can be referred to as physically challenged, or disabled, in response to the negative reference to 'paralyzed' or 'handicapped'. Instead of saying 'deaf, dumb', you can say 'Child with Hearing and Speech Impairment'. Instead of calling them'mentally retarded', it can be said to be a child with a brain defect.Instead of calling them'slow learners', it can be said 'Dyslexic'.

II. Mention children with disabilities on an equal footing with children with no disabilities. For example, a student with a physical disability can teach lessons to a child who is younger than himself or herself, and children with disabilities should interact with children who do not have such disabilities in any way they can.

III. Give children with disabilities the opportunity to express their thoughts and feelings freely. Allow children with disabilities to work with children with disabilities in educational and school-related programs and activities.

IV. Take good care of children and learn from their shortcomings. Early detection of deficiencies is also part of learning at a young age. The sooner we find the defects, the sooner and more effectively we can treat them and reduce the severity of the defects.

V. After finding the defects, arrange for appropriate treatment, tests, etc.

VI. Try to adapt the equipment and classrooms used to teach lessons to suit the use and understanding of children with disabilities. For a child with a visual impairment, writing in large letters can teach lessons, such as sitting in front. Adjust the classroom so that the child with difficulty moving can easily enter. Change course patterns, play, and other activities so that students can develop positive thoughts about disabilities in their minds.

VII. Let their parents, friends, and relatives know what kind of special needs a child with a disability will have. Talk to parents about these things in private and at public events.

VIII. Teach parents who are frustrated with their child's disabilities simple steps on how to properly handle such children. Help them to be patient and avoid bullying their children out of anger.

IX. Guide parents and other family members of a child with a physical disability on how to reduce the risk of parental frustration and depression.

X. Involve the parents of children with disabilities in school-related activities and project decision-making.

Works Cited:

Abrahamson, C. E. (1998). Storytelling as a pedagogical tool in higher education. Education, 118(3), 440-452.

Arskey, H., & O'Malley, L. (2005). Scoping studies: Towards a methodological framework. International Journal of Social Research Methodology, 8(1), 19-32. doi: 10.1080/1364557032000119616

Belet, S. D., &Dala, S. (2010). The use of storytelling to develop the primary school students' critical reading skill: the primary education pre-service teachers' opinions. Procedia-Social and Behavioral Sciences, 9, 1830-1834.

Bromfield, L. M., Gillingham, P., & Higgins, D. J. (2007). Cumulative harm and chronic child maltreatment. Developing Practice: The Child, Youth and Family Work Journal, 19, 34-42.

Campbell Collaboration. (2018). What is a systematic review? Retrieved from https://www.campbellcollaboration.org/research-resources/writing-a-campbell-systematic-review/systemic-review.html

Cremin, T., Mottram, M., Collins, F., Powell, S., & Safford, K. (2009). Teachers as readers: building communities of readers. Literacy, 43(1), 11-19.

Dugan, J. (1997). Transactional literature discussions: Engaging students in the appreciation and understanding of literature. The Reading Teacher, 51(2), 86-96.

Ellis, G., & Brewster, J. (2014). Tell it again!: the storytelling handbook for primary english language teachers. London: British Council. Penguin Books.

Gilbert, R., Widom, C. S., Browne, K., Fergusson, D., Webb, E., &Janson, S. (2009). Burden and consequences of child maltreatment in high-income countries. The Lancet, 373(9657), 68-81.

Goudvis, A., & Harvey, S. (2000). Strategies that work: Teaching comprehension to enhance understanding. York, ME: Stenhouse.

Haven, K. F., &Ducey, M. (2007).Crash course in storytelling. Boston: Greenwood Publishing Group.

Isbell, R., Sobol, J., Lindauer, L., &Lowrance, A. (2004).The effects of storytelling and story reading on the oral language complexity and story comprehension of young children. Early Childhood Education Journal, 32 (3), 157-163.

Lewin S, Booth A, Glenton C, Munthe-Kaas H, Rashidian A, Wainwright M, ... Noyes J. (2018). Applying GRADE-CERQual to qualitative evidence synthesis findings: introduction to the series. Implementation Science, 13(Suppl 1)(2), 1-10.

Miller, S., &Pennycuff, L. (2008). The power of story: Using storytelling to improve literacy learning. Journal of Cross-Disciplinary Perspectives in Education, 1(1), 36-43.

Moher, D., Stewart, L., &Shekelle, P. (2015). All in the family: Systematic reviews, rapid reviews, scoping reviews, realist reviews, and more. Systematic Reviews, 4(1), 183.

Remenyi, D. (2005). Tell me a Story–A way to Knowledge. The Electronic Journal of Business Research Methodology, 3(2), 133-140.

Roller, M. R., &Lavrakas, P. J. (2015).Applied qualitative research design: A total quality framework approach. New York: Guilford Publications.

Soleimani, H., &Akbari, M. (2013). The effect of storytelling on children's learning English vocabulary: A case in Iran. International Research Journal of Applied and Basic Sciences, 4(11), 4005-4014.

Stoltenborgh, M., Bakermans-Kranenburg, M. J., Alink, L. R., &IJzendoorn, M. H. (2015). The prevalence of child maltreatment across the globe: Review of a series of meta-analyses. Child Abuse Review, 24(1), 37-50.

Straková, Z. (2011). Using Storytelling with Intensive Reading in Adult Classes (Doctoral dissertation).Retrieved from University Masarykova). (Access No. 104497).

Ta'amneh, M. I. (2018, September) The Effect of Using Storytelling on Developing Saudi EFL University Students' Reading Comprehension. Journal of Education and Practice, 9, 80-87.

Thorpe, D. (1994). Evaluating child protection. Buckingham, UK: Open University Press.

Veltman, M. W., & Browne, K. D. (2001). Three decades of child maltreatment research: Implications for the school years. Trauma, Violence, & Abuse, 2(3), 215-239.

CHAPTER THREE

SHORT STORY WRITING: INCEPTION AND DISSEMINATION

The article *Short Story Writing: Inception and Dissemination* explains what a short story is and presents the views of Western scholars on the short story. It also indicates the difference between a novel and a short story and explains the definitions, strategies, style and types of short stories. At last, it seeks to provide a thorough view and understanding of the short story.

People's attention in storytelling has been around for many centuries. In ancient times stories were spread orally. Many people have gathered and enjoyed listening to what someone has to say. Then the story literature was performed in the form of drama. With the advent of the Industrial Revolution and the advent of printing presses, fiction became the new literary genre of novels and short stories. The twentieth century was a time of storytelling. With the advent of magazines, story literature took shape.

Short stories and novels were prominent in the magazine's publication. Short stories have a unique place in the literary world today. The development of academic knowledge and the development of magazines have fostered an interest in reading among people. The short story is set in a fast-paced modern world. The short stories are short and lively enough to be read even when travelling by train or bus, or from time to time between works.

It is not possible to define exactly what the short story should look like. Because, something beyond that, the definition can give birth to a short story. But even the following explanations will help us to understand what a short story is. The short story should be small in size. It should be able to sit and finish reading once. At the same time, the summary of the novel does not become a short story; it cannot be a chapter of a novel or a branching story extracted from a long story. The form of the short story is an individual piece that is complete in itself. Whatever emotion or idea it possesses, the short story needs the energy to flow like lightning in the heart of the reader. The storyteller's artistry, imagination, rhetoric, and the message he conveys behind the story are far more important than grammatical limits. The best short story writers do not write with any grammar in mind. Their characters take the form of short stories by themselves.

Literary quality short stories can be traced back to the West in the early 19th century. In the United States, Washington Irving, Edgar Allan Poe, Nathaniel Hawthorne, and in Russia, Turgenev and Chekhov, and France, Maupassant have written excellent short stories. The above-mentioned writers and the critics who have examined their works give the following definitions to the short story.

Brander Mathews has defineda short story as a singular form of the name of a new literary form, rather than as a short story. Edgar Allan Poe, in his essay "The Philosophy of Composition," said that a short story should be read in one sitting, anywhere from a half-hour to two hours. H.E. Bates says that the author's courage in writing can be expressed in any way in the short story.

The most popular literary genres today are novels and short stories. Magazines also rely solely on these two genres. The two are similar in some theories and different in many places. It should therefore be clearly understood that the two are different art forms.

Similarities: Both novels and short stories are literary gifts to Tamil from the West. Both novel short stories are in prose form. Both genres are based on the story. Critics, therefore, refer to the two as fictional literature.

Differences: Critics have illustrated the difference between a short story and a novel with some examples. The short story is like a tree whereas the novel is like a grove where many trees thrive. The short story is like a painting in one or two colours whereas the novel is like a giant painting painted in many different colours. The short story is like a bird flying alone whereas the novel is like many birds flying together in a herd. The short story can be considered as a beautiful fragrant single flower whereas the novel can be compared to a garland tied with string.

The short story focuses on a character, an action, or an event in life but the novel covers many traits and events. Showing the different stages of development of life is novel; the short story only shows one dimension of life. In the novel, we can show that the characters are gradually evolving. It is not possible to say so in the short story. The structure and trend of the short story as a whole and the structure and trend of the novel are different.

The short story is born in the mind of the author and ends in the mind of the reader. For the short story, the meaning it speaks of, the time frame, and the unity are very important. The meaning of the short story may vary from writer to writer. Yet they can generalize that society is a novel subject.

Short story writers not only imagine what they see and hear but also polish it like adding copper to gold. Often literature is a mirror that reflects society. Short stories are no exception. The author observes the events going on around him and narrates them. Based on the variations a short story can be classified into three major types. They are The Story of Plot, The Story of Character and The Story of Impression. The theme spoken in the short stories are,

1. Individual problem - based on the problem of the individual, the inner struggle of the individual is given priority.
2. Family problem - based on problems in family life, between husband and wife, between brother and sister, between mother-in-law and daughter-in-law, and between brother-in-law. Female writers are at the forefront of effectively writing such family stories.
3. Social problem - based on child marriage, widow abuse, inappropriate marriage, dowry abuse, caste oppression, untouchability, and superstition.
4. Economic problem - based on the economic struggle, poverty and scarcity that are the daily problems of today's society.
5. Liberation of the country - based on the national liberation struggle of the forties and fifties.

Short stories are also written based on modern scientific ideas and current issues such as sexual violence, eve-teasing, abortion, and the water issue.

There is no time limit for short stories. One can have a period of the short story from birth to death; or a story can be written in a day, in an hour, in a few seconds of one's life. There is no need to tell the time and place of the story at the beginning. As the story unfolds, you can occasionally give hints about time and place. The chronology in the short story should not be too detailed except for one or two series. Mythological and historical periods can also be brought into the short story.

Short stories should run and be completed with complete concentration. The same feeling that is shown at the beginning of the story must grow and complete between the same feeling and the end. Critics refer to this as the Unity of Impression. Next, the purpose for which the author created the short story should be focused. The story should go towards the specific goal and end without distracting the readers' attention and interest in the slightest.

The structure of the short story should be systematic and firm. When a talented writer writes a short story, he does not fabricate ideas for the events of the story. Imagination shows with a deep focus for a conclusion. Although short stories have the same structure as the beginning, climax, and end, they have subtle differences among themselves. Title, beginning and end have an essential place in the short story system. A good name is essential for a short story. The appropriate name and its charm make readers want to read. The uniqueness of the short story author lies in the search for a name. The short titles of the short story should cover the big gist of the story.

Critics divide the title of the short story into four categories. They are,

1. The title that holds the beginning of the story
2. The title that holds the object of the claim
3. The title that holds the name of the central character
4. The title on which the end is made.

The beginning of the short story should be lively and motivate the reader to read. Better a poor horse than no horse at all. The beginning of the short story should appear in our minds as a gallop. The beginning of the short story should be thrilling; you need to drag them out in the middle of a show before they get bored. It should catch the reader's attention at the beginning of the story. Otherwise set aside that the story is not tasty. Short stories generally thrive when they have a good beginning for the plot and plot.

As mentioned above, the beginning of the short story should attract the readers like a magnet and motivate them to read above without scattering the thought.

The end of the short story was expected to be pleasant in the early days of short story development. Many authors are satisfied with the end of the story. But it is a weakness. Life is not always happy; there was crying, too, and it was said that tragic results must be acknowledged. A story does not have a beautiful ending or tragic ending. Whichever of these is perceived as the right and appropriate decision, only then can the story succeed. The climax and ending of the story are located together in some stories. That is, the input of the story reaches full clarity at the climax as well as the story ends. The climax and ending are the same in a story that revolves around the same character. Often, the story should end briefly in a couple of sentences after reaching its climax.

In today's literary world, there is a distinct place for short stories. Millions of people are involved in reading. Even with the advent of radio, film, television, and video, reading habits have not diminished. This is because of the creativity of our short story writers. One of the reasons is that it is easy to read not only in leisure time but also in travel time. It is for this reason that short story reading has increased today more than ever before than the novel.

Works Cited:

1. Collie, J. & S. Slater.*Literature in the Language Classroom: A Resource Book of Ideas and Activities*. Cambridge: Cambridge University Press. 1987.
2. Durham, M. K. *Creative writing*. 13(1), 155-174, 1970.
3. Erkaya, O. *Benefits of Using Short Stories in the EFL Context*. Asian EFL Journal, 2005.
4. Harmer, J. *How to teach writing*. Pearson Education Limited, Malaysia. 2004.

Saricoban, A., &Kucukoglu, H. *Using literature in EFL class: short story*. 1st International Conference on Foreign Language Teaching and Applied Linguistics. May 5-7 2011 Sarajevo. 2011.

CHAPTER FOUR

WRITING NOVELS: INCEPTION AND INTERROGATION

The article *Writing Novels: Inception and Interrogation* explains the origin, definition and characters of the novel. Also, it elucidates the social reasons for the emergence of the novel with how the elements of the novel, the theme, the plot, the characterization, the stream of consciousness, the dialogue, the context, the style are all function.

English literature is great literature of old and new. Among these, old literary forms such as epics, long narrative poems, devotional songs, etc. are still used today. At the same time, new genres such as short stories, novels, biographies, etc. bring the flavour. Old literature appeared long ago while the new literature appeared later. Thus, even if these are divided into two, there is no doubt that they are identical in taste and usefulness.

In the beginning, many pieces of literature were created in the form of poems. These days, they are graded in prose form. Previously, written as long poems *Iliad* and *Odyssey* etc but novels that are currently being written into long stories. In both, the story, the narration, and the characters are considered to be works of art. This section introduces the novel, one of the most popular contemporary literary forms. Also, it introduces its structure, definition, characterization, strategy, and expressiveness in general.

Fiction is a general term for literary genres such as novel and short story. Fiction is different from traditional folk tales. Creativity was shaped in the form of prose only after the arrival of the West. The missionaries, who wanted to spread their religion among the people, began to use prose to make it easier for spreading their doctrines. This change also began to appear in literary genres. In that way, fiction flourished as prose literature.

Storytelling and listening are human characteristics. It is an ancient form of entertainment found in all centres of human civilization. The curiosity to know what is going to happen next is what causes the story to appear. The novel is a long story in prose that explains human relationships, thoughts and actions.

The word novel means 'new'focused on world experience. It is derived from the Italian word 'Novella'. Many scholars have interpreted the novel in different ways. It is an interpretation of human life in prose narrative style that gave birth to the Neo-Renaissance in English prose.

The novel first appeared in Italy. It was mostly depicting romantic events. So the word 'novel' was originally given the meaning of Romance. Only later did it become a form of savouring human life. Samuel Richardson wrote the novel, *Pamela*,in 1741. This is considered to be the first novel in the English language. One of the benefits of the arrival of the British to India was the development of prose with the help of the printing press they introduced. Its expression is the literary form of the novel.

The novel develops the story by leaving many branches like a tree. It can be read for many hours. There may be many short stories in the novel. Thus the short story cannot be considered as a novel if many are added. The novel has a large field of its own. In short, the novel has a great story and many storytellers depicting many areas of individual or community life. The field of the novel is the appropriate place to depict this. The story is the setting for the novel, the screen for the painting and the stage for the dance. The novel usually has a 'theme'. The plot should be natural. Anything can be the theme of the novel. It takes on the form of a beautiful novel with its performances, the emotions of the storytellers, the imagination and the openness of the narrative. The novel is composed of plot, storytelling, character creation, dialogue, conscious technique, visual, narrative, and style.

A novel needs a story and the theme is essential to art. There is no justice in the fact that 'this is' the theme of the novel. The storyline can come from anywhere; may come at any time. That is what the artist sees the world as. Any major event in human life, historical facts, everyday life, psychological issues can be the subject of the novel. The best strategy is to embed the plot in the story so that the learner can count and realize himself.

The story is a chronological sequence of events. Plot refers to the causal relationship between sequential events. The events in the story should occur naturally, not as if they were coming suddenly. The tendency of novels is for shows to expand and grow according to the story and to achieve fulfilment. Based on nature, the plot can be classified into two major categories. They are Loose Plot and Organic Plot.

A loose plot means that the events in the story are unrelated or irrelevant. The protagonist will be the central character in all the episodes and will connect the other characters of the story. In this type of novels, only the characterization is given special attention.

Each story in the organic plot is interrelated. The end of one episode will lead to the start of the next. The novels set in this will be lively. In some places, it is found unreliable. Historical and detective novels are the best evidence for this plot. The plot should work as it should. None of its eyes should appear artificial. The methods used to create the storyline must be credible and acceptable. Among the novels with the best storytelling structure, Suspense and Irony etc. are located. It is only when these are directed forward that the novel acquires beauty.

The novel should not deliberately create unexpected events, or show all of a sudden coincidence. These are not desirable. The characters in the story will speak and the author will speak. In these speeches, there will be an object. Inside, the crypt has still located an object. This is called Irony. Sometimes this explicit object is one and the object of reference is the opposite.

The social background and ecosystem play an important role in the novel. That is, the time and place in which the novel takes place is the context. It is in this area that people's lives, their customs, etc. take place. The situation should be set according to where the story is said to take place. A novelist claims that storytelling that takes place in the villages should not go into the old-fashioned way of painting mansions and even towers. The context can be divided into (1) Social setting and (2) Material setting. In some novels, only a section of society serves as the background. The background of the novel could be the life of the upper class, the life of the middle class, the life of the grassroots or the life of the workers. Habits, lifestyles, etc. are the categories of social background. Some novelists describe streets, houses, interiors, etc. in great detail with systematic features. Landscaping is the background of some other renowned novelists. Thus nature is used in many ways in novels. Let them come;

(1) The use of nature as a mere cosmetic without any connection with human activity.

(2) The use of nature in direct relation to human activity.

Based on the theme and plot there are five major types of characters in fiction. There might be more types of novel, poem, drama, epic, etc are concerned but as far as short stories are concerned, the following characters are significant.

1. Flat character

2. Round character

3. Dynamic character

4. Static character

5. Stereotypical or stock character

Flat character: This character does not essentially change throughout the story. E.g. supporting characters. It is also called type character.

Round character:A round character has something of the complexity, we find in real human beings. He or she changes in some important way as the novel or story unfolds itself and stands out. This character is usually individualistic and recognized by his particular merits or faults, which bring development in the story. E.g. Protagonist.

Dynamic character:A dynamic character is a character, which changes significantly during the story. These changes include changes in insight or understanding, values, Changes in commitment. Changes in circumstances do not apply unless they result in some change within the character's self. E.g. The Protagonist is always nearly a dynamic character. Antagonists sometimes are dynamic as well.

Static character:A static character does not undergo significant change. Whether round or flat, their personalities remain essentially stable throughout the story. This is commonly done with secondary characters to let them serve as thematic or plot elements. E.g. supporting characters and major characters other than the protagonist are generally static.

Stereotypical or stock characters: These characters are often the basis of flat characters, though elements of stock characters can be found in round characters also. They do not change throughout the story. This gives a brief idea about the art of characterization in a short story and also tells how characterization contributes to making a short story interesting and finally popular by touching the heart of the reader.

The author employs several stratagems to make the reader enjoy reading the novel. Notable among them is the Stream of Consciousness. Character traits can be seen in novels through a new technique called Stream of Consciousness. It is the process of forming thoughts that arise from within, from one, and the other. There will be no match between these thoughts. The strategy of the Stream of Consciousness novel is to arrange the thoughts in the way they arise from within. This technique is used to create characters that transcend time and space in two ways. As the X-ray image reveals the internal organs of the body, the novels of consciousness highlight the inner workings of the mind. The English novel *Ulysses*, by James Joyce, is hailed as one of the finest examples for the Stream of Consciousness.

The author expresses his uniqueness through dialogue and language style. The dialogues in the novel should express the nature and characteristics of the story. Any part of the dialogue should be conducive to the narration or development of the story. The conversation should not take place in a way that bores the reader of the novel. The dialogue should be tailored to the plot, the practice, the place where they live, the context in which they act the course of the episode, etc.

Style is a unique way in which an author expresses himself, through his thoughts and focus. The style of the two writers is not the same. Although the writer's style is unique, it should not be forgotten that it is due to his social background. Style in fiction refers to the traditions that are manipulated to make the story various linguistic levels. By controlling one's rhetoric, a writer can control and manipulate various syntax structures, sequences, dialogue, and other elements of language. A special part of the style is vocabulary or dictation. This is the word choice. Words can be selected formally, informally, or in colloquial speech. We find the formal case in academic texts and research papers. Informal word usage can be found in casual conversations and humorous writing. The word rhetoric also refers to the set of words used by the narrator. The rhetoric of some authors would be excellent. Some do not. Style is considered to be an essential element of literature. A good style has to carry the reader with the author until the last without getting bored.Through this article, we could understand the origin of stories. Also, we have come to know that fiction is a general term that refers to both literary genres, novel and short story.

Works Cited:

1. Lamott A. *Bird by Bird: Some Instructions on Writing and Life*. New York: Pantheon Books.735280, 1994.
2. McDonnell M. J. 'Journal of Urban Ecology: Linking and Promoting Research and Practice in the Evolving Discipline of Urban Ecology', Journal of Urban Ecology, 1: 1–6. 2015.
3. *Mind Map,* from Wikipedia. <http://en.wikipedia.org/wiki/Mind_map> accessed 21 November 2017.
4. Strunk W., White E. B., Angell R. *Elements of Style*, 4th edn. Boston: Pearson Education. 1999.

Zinsser W. *On Writing Well,* 30th Anniversary Edition: The Classic Guide to Writing Nonfiction. New York: Harper Collins. 2006.

CHAPTER FIVE

DEATH AS THE MOST CERTAIN POSSIBILITY IN THOMAS NASHE'S POEM, "A LITANY IN TIME OF PLAGUE"

Abstract:

No one in this world, whether rich or poor, wants death. The reason is desire, the desire of deciding to live in this world for some more time. But everything in this world cannot stay here permanently. It is this corona that has made the man realize the unstable nature of life. What we are talking about is today's event, but the poem which is about to be analysed in this article was written centuries ago. This poem, *A Litany in Time of Plague* by Thomas Nashe communicates us the inherent truth about death. It would be horrible to think of people who died of the disastrous plague after the Poet's day, like today's Corona.

This research essay captures the inner essence of the poet's mind and moves towards the conclusion that death will never leave a human being. The man must taste the taste of death. Death is the only sure thing, the most certain possibility. The article ends with the implication that there is no way out of man's escape from death.

Keywords: Thomas Nashe, Litany, Death, Almighty, Pandemic

The Poet in the period of Pandemic:

Many poets have drawn voluminous poems in today's pandemic context. All these poems unite us literally. Through these poems, poets present people with a new form of reality. Many people are looking for a new enjoyment during this time of incarceration. The poems of these poets are in such a way to quench their thirst. The pandemic period is neither today nor day before yesterday. It has hit people many times over the centuries. In such cases, the role of the poets has much to do with the uniformity of literature. In that way, the role of Black Death, the most deadly pandemic of the time of the Elizabethan age, is indispensable. In this article, we are narrating about the life of the poet Thomas Nashe and his contribution to the development of English literature through dramas.

Thomas Nashe was born at Lowestoft, England in 1561, and completed his studies at John's College, Cambridge University, in 1586. He then incorporated himself into a literary circle known as the University Wits, which was very popular during the reign of Queen Elizabeth I. All of the University staged countless plays and composed several poems that had made the English literary world better. Others minor writers wrote and sent articles to newspapers. Our poet Nashe was doing great work then.

In his days, two religious groups were living in England. They were Anglicans and Puritans in major and Catholics as minorities. Several Puritan writers put countless attacks on Anglicans through their criticism. He responded to all of them through satires in the form of Pamphlets. The most important of them is *An Almond for a Parrat*. Our poet has authored many valuable literary works that have a special place in English literature. His famous picaresque novel, *The Unfortunate Traveler*, is still relevant today. He has described countless adventures in that literature. All of those adventures refer not only the English landscapes but the entire European continent. He who composed so many literary works died at the age of 34 years. The death of our poet remains a mystery to this day. Some say he died of Plague and some go with food poisoning.

***A Litany*: Influx and Influence:**

An excellent Elizabethan comedy was staged in the year of 1592. Its name is *Summer's Last Will and Testament*. In that comedy, the poem *A Litany in Time of Plague* was a prayer. When this drama was staged, there had been an unexpected pandemic in England. By then, the plague had threatened entire England through death. All were dying without the discrimination of the rich and poor. Almost one-third of the population died of the plague. The plague, which lasted more than a century, killed 200 million people. This is also called Black Death (Snowden 36). It is to be noted that the then Queen Elizabeth I led her life very carefully since there were no drugs available for the disease. Nashe had always been a devout Anglican and showed loyalty towards Catholic. As a result, the comedy was composed to entertain his patron the archbishop John Whit-gift of Canterbury. The archbishop was then in his hometown with his disciples. He could not return to

London. The cause was a plague. So he staged the play to entertain him. Only in the year 1600, the play was formally registered in London.

The Significance of the Signifiers in the Song:

Today, there are countless researches that give innumerable thoughts to common people. There has been a reliable relation between a social change and an epidemic since Blackdeath. These horrific pandemics starting from Blackdeath to Covid19 do not only transform this society but ultimately lead us to the path of well-being. These pandemics have greatly contributed to the development of not only medicine and public health but also various arts and ideas. An examination of this human history reveals the origins and impacts of countless infectious diseases such as measles, cholera and tuberculosis. Most recent diseases, such as AIDS, SARS and Ebola, have terrified people. The main reason for this is the lack of proper vaccines or medicines for the current diseases such as AIDS, SARS and Ebola. So far, the COVID 19 virus of the SARS family has astounded the world through countless changes. Economics, tourism, the arts and literature, science and philosophy have been questioned. So seeing this present impact, it is somewhat difficult for us to know what happened four hundred years ago. Our poet expresses his opinion through a beautiful song. The following article will clearly show its meaning and aesthetics (Snowden 04).

This poem *A Litany in the Time of Plague* could be considered as one of the most cardinal songs in English Literature. The 'litany' is nothing but a song recited by the Reverend Father. When he recites, people should follow him and recite once again. This poem is deciphered by many scholars in many ways. But if we see this poem as a poem alone, it will emit its true meaning. Here the poet speaks in the form of a dead man. This is true, though somewhat seems contradictory. How did he die? He died of the plague, as we had seen in the previous lines. Going into that corpse, the soul of that poet speaks. It tells people, "Just like I died today, you will die tomorrow." There will be no difference given among those who are going to die. The rich, the poor, the beautiful, the ugly, there will be no discrimination. Death will embrace the people through the plague. And this death will give no escape for man. The final lines of the poem tell us a philosophical truth in a methodological way. The lines convey that death is in the form of plague before our eyes. No matter what you fight, all are equal before death. And this death has no discrimination. There is no mercy. The only essential rule that is written for everyone is 'death'. Even the Savior, Jesus, has met with death. Then how can we humans escape? And as we recite each stanza, we understand that the poet welcomes death. He graciously accepts it. He never feared of death. The reason is our poet has clearly understood the reality of the world. Each passage of the poem clearly shows each page of a man. Each side is filled with that pandemic disease. What we get in the final stanza is that death is the most certain possibility. Those who die will surely get into heaven. And this death to humans is common without discrimination. It cannot be avoided. This earthly death takes us to a new life in a new world which is always eternal.

Death as the Most Certain Possibility:

The Death is the most natural and the most certain entity to all living beings in the world. It is the law which describes us that all that appears in the universe must vanish one day (Heidegger 232). In the same book he also clearly conveys, "In its project it is revealed as something thrown. Thrown and abandoned to the world, it falls prey to it in taking care of it" (Heidegger 232). What Heidegger says is true. The reason is that there are countless differences between animals and humans. One of the most important reasons among them is the way of life. Only man has to be taught to live. Other organisms such as birds, animals and insects can lead their lives without any parental care. Some basic functions such as how to talk to others, how to eat food, how to walk and how to swim, etc, because he was just thrown into this world. The world is awe for him who has just come out of his mother. Awe and fear frighten him. In fact, that fear alone makes him live. He fears of death. He wonders and contemplates on how death will appear to him. His soul does not want to accept the pain of death. In general, Man meets his own death through five different ways such as natural death, accident, murder, suicide, and natural disasters. It is also to be noted that man does not show any interest to meet his own death from those five. Instead, he wants only to live. Unfortunately, he can't stay in this world forever. There are so many problems are waiting to chase him. He must overcome all those mysteries. Although he may have won many of those mysteries, there is no escape from the mystery of death. Because no one knows how death will get close to him. Now, what is the situation today? What is going on in the world? Why do thousands of people die every day? Who brought this Corona into the world? What is the need for it? How does it differ from others? In fact, this Coronavirus has a unique character because it is not easy for us to state whether death through this Coronavirus is a murder, suicide, accident, natural death and natural disaster. It is all. With the advent of this, many of the superpowers have gone unnoticed today. Humans have given up the desire to live. Siddhas and Mukhtas called the death a natural phenomenon. Saints, yogis and sages all did something to overcome death. But death could not be won. Buddha, Mahavira, Jesus, Mohammed, Raman, Sankara, Ramanujar are all dead. Death has been a mystery to man since the world began. No one has unravelled the puzzle yet. Is there rebirth after death? Some people say yes and some say no. Somehow the answer to this question has not been answered yet. Scriptures, Vedantas and ideologies were written to explain the relationship among man, the world, the cosmos, and God (Rao 127). In total, the litany comprises of six kinds of dissimilar meanings in all six stanzas. In the first stanza, the poet welcomes death. The second stanza speaks of the notion that death is impartial and belongs to everyone. The third stanza describes the transitory state of beauty. The fourth stanza is about the mortality of heroism, the fifth is about the fading forms of the intellectuals, and finally the sixth emphasizes the world as a stage. This is what the English dramatist Shakespeare speaks in his famous *All the World is a Stage.*

Valediction to the Uncertain:

The poet Nashecomposed the litany in a plain language without bombastic lines or flowery words. This poem was written in the time of Queen Elizabeth I. It was also not so familiar to compose simple poems by the sophisticated poets like the University Wits. Then why did he compose this poem in such a simple way? Because he's a genius. He was very clear that everyone should understand his view of death. He said that death would treat all classes equally. And the words he uses are very common. The reason is that death should be simple and understandable to the common man also. The audience could easily sense the desire of Nashe for the consciousness of embracing the death as an inevitable phenomenon from the following stanza.

Adieu, farewell, earth's bliss;
This world uncertain is;
Fond are life's lustful joys;
Death proves them all but toys;
None from his darts can fly;
I am sick, I must die.
Lord, have mercy on us!

The poet's thought appears to us in the first stanza of this song. Here, death is deeply ingrained in him. And he says that man's life in this world is absolutely uncertain. There are innumerable joys and countless sorrows before this death but in reality, he can't escape from the death and no matter how many sins and goods he has committed. Death is a primordial thing. It doesn't have any past and future. The poet utters that if there is an end to all suffering in this world; it is possible only by death. He also states that no one can escape from the crucifixion of death. And to say that one's death is better than living at anguish and agony. It is better to die than to live with a disease every day. And the last two lines of this first stanza appear throughout all the passages of this poem. He welcomes death. And that death should be only from the lord in heaven. So death cannot be deceived by man. Dying is safer than suffering. Only the Lord Almighty can take his people to the eternal world where we find no death, no pain, no cry, no sorrow and no hunger. So, the poet requests the lord almighty to offer death.

Money Alone Cannot Buy Happiness:

Rich men, trust not in wealth,
Gold cannot buy you health;
Physic himself must fade.
All things to end are made,

The plague full swift goes by;
I am sick, I must die.
Lord, have mercy on us!

Death caused by the fatal disease does not know the difference between the rich and the poor. There we find equality and absolute socialism. This absolute equality can be found only with God. All are equal to God. Everyone in the world is his children. We cannot find God in prejudice. So the poet gives some advice to the rich. He tells the rich men not to flee in vain but to seek man. Neither gold nor money would give him the means to escape from the disease. Whatever we have, they must die or vanish. This applies to all living beings and non-living beings. This earth will go away from the solar system one day. The sun will get sink into the darkness one day, and the stars will disappear one by one. The good health of the rich men will eventually shrink. Everything created in this world has to die one day. Whether it is soil or mountain, whether a small insect or a large elephant, Death is certain. So man is not far off. The man will die all at once in a single attack of that infection. So death cannot be deceived by man. Dying is safer than suffering. Only the Lord Almighty can take his people to the eternal world where we find no death, no pain, no cry, no sorrow and no hunger. So, the poet requests the lord almighty to offer death.

Beauty is Untruth, Untruth Beauty:

Beauty is but a flower
Which wrinkles will devour;
Brightness falls from the air;
Queens have died young and fair;
Dust hath closed Helen's eye.
I am sick, I must die.
Lord, have mercy on us!

This third stanza explains to us how beauty embraces death. Each organism has its own duration. Man has a maximum of 100 years or at least 60, a day for Mayflies and more than a century for turtles. A tree is a seed that has got emerged from a seed. Then it grows. There will be a flower in that plant. The flower then becomes a fruit, and after that, the fruit is ripened and will be leaving the tree. Here the tree which was left could be considered as the world. Then the man eats that fallen fruit, and He too starts growing up to be an infant and eventually dies as an old man. So the death doesn't differentiate good or bad, king or queen, and Helen or Cleopatra. So the beauty of one's outlook is always a vincible factor. Later, the fire and worms consume the human body. Now the beautiful body will soon become an earthy part with soil. Then a new creature emerges from the soil again. Hence, the role of death is always seen as a crucial one in maintaining this everlasting cycle in the universe. So death cannot be deceived by man. Dying is safer than suffering. Only the Lord Almighty can take his people to the eternal world where we find no death, no pain, no cry, no sorrow and no hunger. So, the poet requests the lord almighty to offer death.

The Valiant too tastes of Death:

Strength stoops unto the grave,
Worms feed on Hector brave;
Swords may not fight with fate,
Earth still holds open her gate.
'Come, come!' the bells do cry.
I am sick, I must die.
Lord, have mercy on us!

What about the superpower countries like the US and the UK? What's the use of having atomic bombs? It is not even a possible task to destroy a small virus. This is the law of nature which cannot be rewritten. Nature itself has no power to control or alter its own decision to kill someone. Rarely, we could postpone our death. Postponing the death can be possible, but Postponing permanently is not. All the great heroes of the ancient world are sleeping peacefully today. Hercules, Hector, Achilles, Odysseus, Ajax, Menelaus, Agamemnon, Priam and Paris, are the instant instances. They have become soiled with soil. Death has taken them to the world of eternal happiness. It is also waiting to take many more from here. So having a sword fight with that death can never be won. A hero can beat another by standing face to face. But how can he overcome the invisible? .Here it is not only invisible but also highly infectious. An invisible person can easily bring us down. There will be more heroes coming and going in this world. But staying permanently is impossible. So death cannot be deceived by man. Dying is safer than suffering. Only the Lord Almighty can take his people to the eternal world where we find no death, no pain, no cry, no sorrow and no hunger. So, the poet requests the lord almighty to offer death.

The Witty! Settle thy Studies:

Wit with his wantonness
Tasteth death's bitterness;
Hell's executioner
Hath no ears for to hear
What vain art can reply.
I am sick, I must die.
Lord, have mercy on us!

The fifth stanza is somewhat strange to be interpreted. What we see in this stanza are two kinds of death. One is heavenly death and the other is satanic death. How is this possible? Delightful death can only be offered by the Almighty Lord, the Father of Heaven. But the painful death can only be delivered by Satan, the ruler of Hell. Take, for instance, Dr.Faustus. He fell into the trap of Lucifer through disrespecting God and started learning unwanted things through Mephistopheles. Whenever we break a rule, our destiny ends. When we do not respect destiny, how can only destiny respect us? All the wise men who left their life in the world had already thought about the pattern of death through different designs. It is extended from Socrates to Sartre. Whatever the case, no man can ever win death. We do not know from which direction death comes from. The last minutes of a man's death can only be emotionally experienced but not to be intellectually comprehended because the thoughts of each thinker are different. So death by Satan is the most tormenting and tantalising but the death, available through the Almighty Lord, will lead us to eternal life. So these two types of death have no eyes and ears. Whether rich or poor, there can be no discrimination. A pandemic virus can kill both a scavenger and a doctor. A contagious virus can kill both the judge and koyambedu market labourers. If we start to think about how it is possible, then we have to face death as soon as possible because we can't answer to certain things. The most important part of those few is death. Even if we think about it, death will soon catch us. It is unnecessary. For what? We can't do anything against it. Then why should we think about it? Death never dies. Everything in this universe will die except death. So death cannot be deceived by man. Dying is safer than suffering. Only the Lord Almighty can take his people to the eternal world where we find no death, no pain, no cry, no sorrow and no hunger. So, the poet requests the lord almighty to offer death.

Salvation in Heaven:

Haste, therefore, each degree,
To welcome destiny;
Heaven is our heritage,
Earth but a player's stage;
Mount we unto the sky.
I am sick, I must die.
Lord, have mercy on us!

In this final stanza, we are going to focus on death's innermost intuition rather than its feisty face. Death might be portrayed gravely in the above passages but here the nature of it is quite different. Death seems to be a promising person here. So what our poet wants us to do is to welcome our destiny. We have to welcome our destiny with open arms. The heavenly life of our Father's is more of a place for people than this worldly life. That is permanent. What we currently have is just a stage. When the play is over, we have to go back to our house. There is no death in the place of God where the angels alone can reside. There we can live our life without death since death can never reign over the Lord. The reason is that he has no beginning and no end. Then how could the death embrace the father in heaven? So in this worldly life, we must first win over death. Death alone can help us to overcome death to see all the heights of the sky. Death alone is peace, death alone is meditation, and death alone is a pleasure. Now to lead our life peacefully, there is only one way which is death. So death cannot be deceived by man. Dying is safer than suffering. Only the Lord Almighty can take his people to the eternal world where we find no death, no pain, no cry, no sorrow and no hunger. So, the poet requests the lord almighty to offer death.

If there is a central motif in this song, it is only death. No one can escape from the clutches of that natural death. It will kill everyone without discriminating against the rich and poor. The cause of death in this poem is due to an epidemic. No mortal can escape, overcome, or escape from death. So in this short period of time in this world, we have to live without suffering. Death can take us out of this world at any time. When that death comes to call us, we should not fear it. Rather, we should gladly welcome it to live a sustainable life. This poem can be interpreted in countless terms. But if we look into our inner gaze, only death is visible. The beauty of death is revealed when we look closely at this poem. Sometimes death can scare us with its grotesque face. We should not regret it. In fact, death alone is the most certain possibility of a human being. Coronavirus to date has killed more than 200 thousands of people. Likewise, the Elizabethan poem had seen the deaths of some 200 million people. Only through such deaths, people of all countries in Europe gather together (Sloane 09). They start acting in unison. The ultimate purpose of the poem was to create a clear understanding of death through the death point of view itself.

Works Cited:

1. Heidegger, Martin. *Being and Time*. State University of New York Press, 1996.
2. Nashe, Thomas. “A Litany in the Time of Plague.” *Poetry Foundation*, www.poetryfoundation.org/poems/50660/in-time-of-plague-adieu-farewell-earths-bliss Accessed 21April 2020.
3. Rao, B.V. *World History from Early Times to AD 2011*. Sterling Publishers Pvt. Ltd, 2017.

4. Snowden, Frank. *Epidemics and Society: From the Black Death to the Present*. Yale University Press, 2019.
5. Sloane, Barnie. *The Black Death in London*. The History Press, 2011.

9 798885 030090

Printed by Libri Plureos GmbH in Hamburg, Germany